KV-373-962

THE BLACK KNIGHT

An exciting historical adventure

through the Middle Ages

THE BLACK KNIGHT

by Michael Thomson

Illustrated by Bryony Jacklin

To my nephews, Alexander and Gabriel, with love.

The Black Knight
LD 954
ISBN 1 85503 137 X
© Text Michael Thomson
© Illustrations Bryony Jacklin
All rights reserved
First published 1992

LDA, Duke Street, Wisbech, Cambs PE13 2AE,
England

Printed in Great Britain by
Ebenezer Baylis & Son Ltd,
The Trinity Press, Worcester, and London

READ THIS FIRST!

You are the star in this adventure story. You begin in the year 2167, when time machines were invented. You are in the Time Patrol which looks after Time and makes sure that History isn't changed. Evil enemies of the Future like Brodric are travelling through time to try to change History. If they succeed, they will be able to rule the world. Your job is to stop them.

You will need a copy of the Adventure Sheet at the back of this book. (You can write in this book if it is your book. If not, ask someone to photocopy the Adventure Sheet for you.) You also need two dice and a pencil.

As you travel through Time in this adventure you will meet many people and find out about the times they live in. You will also meet many enemies of the Future. You will have to fight them. When you fight you will throw your dice and work out your fighting skills. The story will tell you when to fight.

Look at the Adventure Sheet. It lists all the enemies you may have to fight. Every time you fight someone remember to fill in your Adventure Sheet. This is how you do it:

> *Every time the story tells you to prepare for battle, you need to throw the two dice. Write the number of the dice throw in the adventure sheet in the 'Dice throw' column alongside the name of the enemy. Then add the dice throw to the number in the column called 'Your Skill points'. This number is your total Fighting Skill points. Write this number in the column called 'Your total Fighting Skill points'. The story gives you the enemy's Fighting Skill points. Write this number in the column called 'Enemy's Fighting Skill points'. You win the battle if you have the same as or more Fighting Skill points than the enemy. You lose if you have fewer Fighting Skill points than the enemy.*

The Adventure Sheet also shows you that you have 25 Life Points. You may lose Life Points in the adventure. You may also be given some. Be careful, if you lose all your Life Points you die!

At the back of the book is another important part of your adventure – your Equipment List. You can also get this photocopied if you need to. In your adventure you will find or be given things that will help you. You must write them down on your Equipment List. Write down the story number you are on as well so you can find it again when you need it. If you do not have the right equipment you will have to go back to find it.

To begin the adventure start at the story number with **1** at the top. You will be told what to do next at the end of the story number. Now read on.

GOOD LUCK!

1

A strange hum fills the air. Lights flash on the panel in front of you. You can smell something hot and burning! Suddenly a bell rings. You turn towards the noise. You see a small launch pad. It is about the size of a car but it is empty. Then the air seems to thicken. An odd-looking machine starts to appear. It is a bit like a car without wheels. It floats in the air and has a cockpit like an aeroplane. Inside the cockpit sits a young woman. In front of her are banks of levers, dials, flashing lights and knobs. The Time Machine has returned!

'Hello, Jane!', you say as she climbs out of the Time Machine. 'How did it go?'

Jane is dressed in long, flowing robes and looks like a Roman. This is because she has just come back from Roman times! 'I have finished my main task. The good news is that Julius Caesar will still invade Britain in 55 BC!', she replies. 'The bad news is that Brodric escaped me! I'm going to report to the Time Leader now. Coming?' Go to **2**.

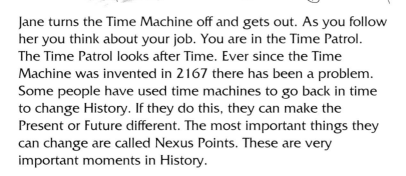

2

Jane turns the Time Machine off and gets out. As you follow her you think about your job. You are in the Time Patrol. The Time Patrol looks after Time. Ever since the Time Machine was invented in 2167 there has been a problem. Some people have used time machines to go back in time to change History. If they do this, they can make the Present or Future different. The most important things they can change are called Nexus Points. These are very important moments in History.

You think about what the Time Leader said when you were training. 'You see, if someone goes back to an event in the Past they can change Now! So if someone went back in Time and killed your grandparents you would not be alive now! History must be kept as it was. Who knows what awful things there might be if the Past was changed?'

Brodric is one of the evil people who plan to change History. He and people like him want to alter the Present and the Future. If they succeed, they will be able to rule the world. Your job as a member of the Time Patrol is to stop them.

You go into the Time Leader's room. Jane makes her report and finishes by saying, 'I think that Brodric plans to go to a Nexus Point in the Middle Ages of British History. I heard him say that the Black Knight would destroy the Time Patrol!'.

The Time Leader turns to you. 'You must find out about the Black Knight!'

Go to **17** if you will or **6** if you will not.

3

You choose to be a Squire. As a squire you are in training to become a knight. You have to look after a knight's weapons and groom his horse. When you get to the armoury you see many weapons. They look like this:

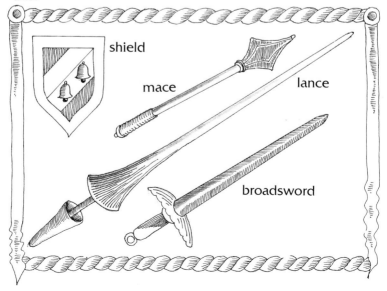

shield

mace

lance

broadsword

You take a lance, a broadsword, a mace and a shield. A lance is a long spear-like weapon for charging (or tilting) at another knight on horseback. A broadsword is a heavy, two-edged sword which you can hold with either hand. A mace is like a steel club which you use to bash at your enemy. A shield is used to protect you from your enemy. A knight usually has his 'coat of arms' on his shield. The coat of arms shows the knight's symbol, family motto or mascot. Write down *Weapons* on your Equipment List. Draw and colour in your own coat of arms on the blank shield below.

You will not be able to fight the Black Knight as a squire. You need to choose again if you are to fight him in the tournament. When you have looked at the picture of the weapons, go to **119** and choose again.

4

You try to dodge past the jailer. He slashes out with his knife. It cuts into you and you feel blood flow. Lose two Life Points. Go back to **112** and throw again.

5

One of the baron's men is watching you. He was expecting to win the contest. You have been very foolish. You have forgotten that your skills are from the Future. The man accuses you of being evil. There are no law courts at this time. You will have to stand trial in the Saxon way. You are given a choice of one of three Saxon customs. People gather around to watch. Go to **7**.

6

Your adventure ends here! What a pity. You are sacked from the Time Patrol. (Go to **17** if you change your mind and decide you do want to take up the challenge.)

7

For your trial you can choose from:

- Ordeal by Fire – **118**
- Ordeal by Combat – **99**
- Ordeal by Water – **53**

8

You enter 1066. Just as you are about to go, the Time Leader comes up to you. She says, 'You must make sure that the Normans win the Battle of Hastings. The History of England after this time will be changed if the Normans do not win. Even if it means that you have to make sure that Harold is killed, you must stop History being changed.' You nod and wave goodbye. You switch on the Time Machine. The air around the Time Leader becomes misty. There is a blackness and a rushing noise.

Within seconds you have landed on the Sussex Downs in 1066! You hide the Time Machine and go to join the Normans as they land. They have landed with 696 ships! The ships are full of knights, horses, archers, carpenters, supplies and many other things.

You plan to slip down to the landing area and join the Norman invaders. You hear one of the men say that they are going to put together wooden forts which they have brought to England in pieces in the ships.

One of the men turns to you and asks you to help unload. You have been trained in many languages from different Times. Will you reply in English – go to **93** – or French – **61**?

9

No. The two-finger V sign for victory was not used until the Second World War (1939-1945) by Winston Churchill. Lose one point and go to **73**.

10

You choose to be a Monk. You shave the top of your head, just leaving a ring of hair. You wear a long brown robe with a simple belt. You also wear sandals. Now go to **15**.

11

You gallop towards the Black Knight. You aim your lance at the centre of his breastplate. As you gallop past him his lance misses you by a hair's breadth. Your lance crashes into him. The Black Knight falls to the ground. Add one point to your score.

You stop your horse. You leap off to the ground. Drawing your broadsword you prepare to fight on. Go to **54**.

12

Brodric's men have laid a trap for you. You get to the year 1170 when Thomas a Becket died. You are spotted at once. The Time Patrol man who is locked in the dungeon in Baron Baric's castle would have been able to warn you. You set your Time Machine back to the year 1102. Lose two Life Points and go to **56**.

13

You tell Henry to take a large force of knights in armour but only a few archers. This is not good advice. The French have many more men with horse and lance than the English. Lose one Life Point and go to **96**.

14

You are lucky. As you bring your staff down the man falls. You strike him on the arm. He drops his staff. Go to **30**.

In 1170, monks and nuns live quiet lives in monasteries or nunneries. Most people in the Middle Ages cannot read and write. Monks and nuns help to keep learning alive. They also help the poor and the sick.

You need to join a pilgrimage to Canterbury. First you need to do your work for the day. Just after midnight you go down to the church to say the first prayers. You have another service at dawn and about seven more services during the rest of the day! After a meeting in the chapter house at 8 am you are given your work for the day. You spend some of the time digging in the gardens. Then you peel potatoes in the kitchen. In the afternoon you help the Master Builder.

The master builder is a monk who is in charge of building a new cathedral. He looks over the plans and scratches his head. He mutters to himself. He tells you about his problem.

The master builder has just been to France. He has found out from the French that if you use a new pointed arch you can make a much lighter church with thinner walls.

He shows you the drawings he has done. Look at them and then go to **16**.

16

The master builder wants to build the highest cathedral in England, but he doesn't know how to keep the walls up without making them too thick. He asks if you have any ideas. Do you:

- say you don't know – go to **38**
- tell him to use concrete – **47**
- tell him about a support system that you think might help – **63**

17

You say that you will take up the challenge. You will need to find out about the Times you are going to visit. The Time Patrol has many costumes and clothes for different Times. To do your research, you can go to:

- the Library to find out about the Nexus Point you are going to – **69**
- the Computer Room to check on Nexus Points – **124**
- the Equipment Room to get the equipment you will need for the Nexus Point you are going to – **79**

18

The soldiers are too close! You hide by running down some stone steps into a food store. The soldiers come down the steps. The guard stands and talks to them. He stands just outside the food store. Slowly you reach out and take the key off the guard's belt. The dark and gloomy stairs are only lit by the flame of a torch. No one sees you. The guard decides to join the others in the search for you.

When they have gone you open the dungeon doors. Inside you find Frank, the Time Patrol man. He looks a bit beaten up. You help him up and creep up the stairs. Frank has taken a risk by hiding his Time Machine in another food store. 'I only planned to be in the castle a minute or two,' Frank tells you. 'I wanted to check out the Baron. It may be that he is one of Brodric's men. I was going to find out and then leave at once. But one of the guards saw me. Luckily they do not know who I am.'

You find Frank's Time Machine. Before he goes he gives you a cloth bag. 'Here', he says, 'you might find this useful!'. Then he is gone. He did not even thank you for getting him out of the dungeon! Now you have to do his job for him and check out the Baron. Add two Life Points to your score for helping Frank. Write down *Cloth Bag* on your Equipment List. Now go to **19**.

19

You make your way up the narrow stone steps. It is late in the day now. The people of the castle are going to the Great Hall to have their evening meal.

The Great Hall is a long room with oak planks on the floor. The floor is covered with rushes. People just throw bones and bits of food on to the floor. The rushes are cleared the next day and new ones are put down. Along the sides of the Hall are long tables and benches. At the top is a table set across the room. This is higher than the other tables. Baron Baric and some of his Knights are sitting at this top table.

In the centre of the room is a fire on a stone slab. The smoke goes out through gaps in the roof. There is a great noise of people, dogs and eating. The food is mostly meat such as beef, venison (deer), sheep and pork. A lot of people are singing and they are getting rather drunk on ale and mead. You need to find a way to get nearer to the Baron.

If you have the Cloth Bag (check your Equipment List), go to **20**. If not, go back to **32**.

20

You step into a dark corner of the room. You take out the contents of the Cloth Bag. It is the costume of a Jester. A jester or fool makes people laugh. You put on the outfit. It is a short tunic and tights and it is made up of red, yellow and green squares. You also have a long hat with three bells on it. You walk up to the Baron's table. He looks like someone you know.

You try a few of your best jokes. He sneers. Then his eyes narrow as he looks closely at you. You suddenly see that it is Brodric himself! He has also realised who you are. 'So, the Time Patrol is here', he says to you. His Knights look confused as he laughs. 'While you mess about here my men are at the Nexus Point! They will deal with the murder of Archbishop Becket!'

You have been tricked! As you run to the door to escape Brodric (or is it Baron Baric?), he shouts, 'Take him alive!'. When you get to the door you find two of his guards in your way. They take out their swords. On the wall of the Hall you see some weapons. You grab a battle-axe and charge. Can you escape? Prepare to meet:

BARON'S GUARDS
FIGHTING SKILLS 15

Throw your dice and work out your score. If you win, go to **115**. If you lose, go to **39**.

21

You choose to be a Nun. You cover your head with a white cloth and wear a long black robe. You have a wide white collar over your neck and shoulders. Now go to **15**.

22

You decide to be a Knight. You put on a long leather jacket with iron rings sewn on to it. There is a slit at the bottom of the jacket so that you can sit on a horse. It is called a 'hauberk'. The round helmet has a long nose part. You take a sword and a long shield. Go to **35**.

23

You decide to be a
Lady. You wear two
long tunics held by a
belt of jewels. Under
your cloak you hide
a long dagger and a
bow and arrow. Go
to **35**.

24

You decide to be an Archer. You take a short bow and a set
of arrows. You wear a long leather jacket with some iron
rings sewn into it. It is like the jacket a Knight wears.
Archers do not normally wear these jackets but you think
you may need it. You also take a long dagger. Go to **35**.

25

Lose one Life Point! Robin Hood, if he did exist, would
have lived in the time of King Richard I. He would have
lived while Richard was away at the Crusades and his
brother John was in England. This would have been around
1189-1199, not in the year 1102. Now go to **82**.

You arrive at Bosworth Field in Leicestershire. Do you have the White Rose? Check your Equipment List. If not, go back to **52** and get it and then come back here. The White Rose will mean that you are on the side that wins the battle.

The Battle of Bosworth Field is a key battle for the future of England. The Wars of the Roses have killed off many of the nobles who had a claim to the throne. Now a man of Welsh background called Henry Tudor is making a claim.

You look around the battlefield. The battle tactics have not changed much since the Battle of Agincourt. You hear a loud bang! You turn and see someone using one of the new handguns. They are still uncommon in these Times. They are dangerous to use because they can easily blow up. They also take a long time to reload!

The two sides hack and push at each other. Richard III is not a popular king. Not many of his subjects want to fight for him. Henry's side is winning. Then, all at once, you hear the rat-a-tat-tat of a modern firearm! Go to **34**.

27

The Carl is a skilful fighter. Before you have time to defend yourself his horse crashes into you. You are thrown to the ground. He gives you a terrible blow across the head. You are stunned for a while. Lose three Life Points. When you look up again you see that the Carl is standing in front of Harold. Go to **45**.

Add one Life Point to your score. You take an antibiotic called penicillin to make sure that you don't catch the plague. Then you put penicillin in the people's food. This will fight the bacteria that cause the Black Death. As you leave one house you can hear children singing:

'Ring a ring a roses,
A pocket full of posies,
A-tishoo, a-tishoo,
We all fall down.'

You recognise this nursery rhyme from when you were little. It is a song which began during the Black Death. It is about what happens when someone catches the plague. First you get a red rash like a ring of roses on your skin. You also start to sneeze. Then you get a fever and very painful lumps under your skin which burst and give out pus. You also bleed under the skin and get black sores. The posies in the song refer to the smell of flowers that is linked to the plague. This could be the smell of the plague itself or perfume which people hold to their noses because of the horrible smell of dying all around them. 'We all fall down' is what happens when people die! When you sang this nursery rhyme as a small child in your own time you did not understand the horror of its meaning.

What will you do next? Go to **29** to choose.

You can try to stop the Black Death by using rat poison –
go to **121** – or pig poison – **57**.

30

The man looks so hungry.
Do you have the Bread
and Cheese? Check your
Equipment List. If you do,
he gives you a castle plan.
Write *Castle Plan* on your
Equipment List and go on
to **31**. If you do not have
the Bread and Cheese, go
back to **85**.

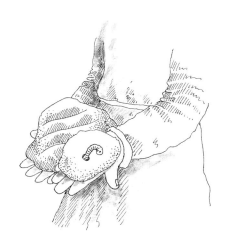

31

At last you come to the
castle of Baron Baric. The
Normans built many
castles to stop the Saxons
rebelling. They were solid,
with square stone walls
and keeps. You enter the
castle by crossing over a
bridge. The bridge has
been lowered down over
a wide stretch of water
which goes right round
the castle. This is called a
moat. You go past the
outer walls that form the
outer bailey. The outer
bailey is a big yard.

The market is held in the castle yard. All around are stables and sheds for corn and hay. There are stalls everywhere and the noise is amazing! You pretend to sell a few beans as you move across the outer bailey. It is not easy to get to the other side because the market is so crowded.

At last you get to the inner wall. The gate is guarded. As the guards look out at the market you slip past. You are now in the inner bailey. This small yard has the keep in it. A keep is a great stone tower, with walls six metres thick! Once again you see that the door is open. You go in. A soldier from the battlement sees you. 'Halt!', he calls.

You run inside. Can you find your way to the dungeons before they catch you? Check your Equipment List. Do you have the Castle Plan? If you do, turn the page and look at the plan. Can you find your way? If not, go back to **30**. If you can, go to **32**.

32

You are lucky that most of the people in the castle are at the market. All you can hear is the sound of running feet as the Norman soldiers chase you.

Just outside the dungeons is a guard. He has the key on his belt but he also has a sword and a dagger. You can:

- try to take the key by force – go to **123**
- try to talk him into giving you the key – **76**
- or hide and wait for the best time to act – **18**

What?! Pray in modern English in the Middle Ages! Lose one Life Point and go back to **107**.

34

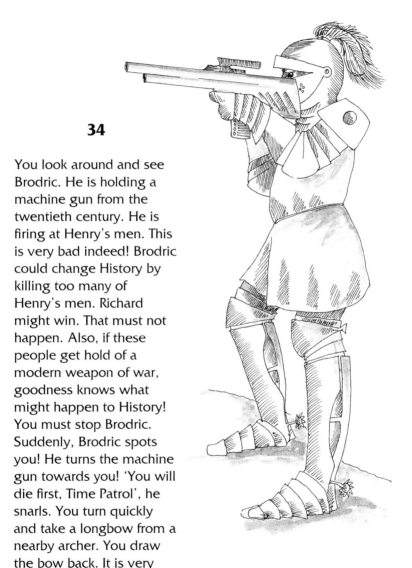

You look around and see Brodric. He is holding a machine gun from the twentieth century. He is firing at Henry's men. This is very bad indeed! Brodric could change History by killing too many of Henry's men. Richard might win. That must not happen. Also, if these people get hold of a modern weapon of war, goodness knows what might happen to History! You must stop Brodric. Suddenly, Brodric spots you! He turns the machine gun towards you! 'You will die first, Time Patrol', he snarls. You turn quickly and take a longbow from a nearby archer. You draw the bow back. It is very difficult! You level the arrow as Brodric aims at you. Go to **49**.

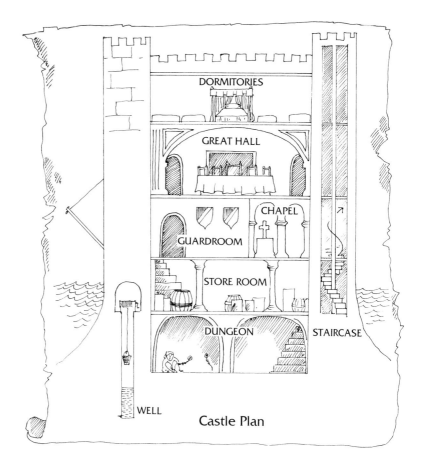

WELL   Castle Plan

35

As you get in the Time Machine you remind yourself that you have been trained in many forms of combat. This makes you feel better. You power up the Time Machine. You look at the flashing date on a dial. You need to set the Time. Set it for one of these years:

- 1170 – go to **87**
- 1066 – go to **8**
- 1415 – go to **74**

(You may need to look at the Middle Ages Time Line again. Check your Equipment List for the number and go back to it if you need to.)

36

The Baker says that he is going on the pilgrimage to make up for his bad deeds. He baked bad bread and was led around the village with bread hanging around his neck. He says that the Archbishop is a good man. The people in the village love him and if he can get Thomas a Becket's blessing in Canterbury they will forgive him.

The Baker drinks rather a lot. Then he starts to pick fights with everyone. At last he falls into a drunken sleep. The Baker's snores keep you awake!

The next day you travel on. Go on to the next evening – **117**.

37

Add one Life Point to your score! Robin Hood, if he did exist, would have lived in the time of King Richard I. He would have lived while Richard was away at the Crusades and his brother John was in England. This would have been around 1189-1199, not in the year 1102. Now go to **82**.

38

You say you do not know. The master builder sends you away in disgust. Lose one Life Point and go back and see him again at **16**.

39

You crash into one of the men. He falls to the ground. You swing the axe around at the other. He ducks and thrusts his sword into your arm. Lose two Life Points. Holding your arm in pain you jump back from his grasp. You run out of the door. Go to **72**.

The longbow is an important weapon. It is used by the yeomen of England. Yeomen and other longbow archers are highly trained. Practising the longbow is a common sport and pastime in these Times. The King and nobles even go so far as to ban football and other sports so that men are trained to use the longbow. English bowmen learn how to fire a bow so that the arrow goes through plate armour. The longbow is as long as the height of the archer. It is made from the wood of the yew tree and has a bowstring made of hemp or flax. The arrows are a metre long and they are made of ash wood and goose feathers. An arrow can kill a man in armour 100 metres away!

Your good advice may help Henry win the Battle of Agincourt. So, to battle! Go to **59**.

41

You gallop towards the Black Knight. You aim your lance at the centre of his breastplate. As you gallop past you miss him by a hair's breadth. The Black Knight's lance crashes into you. The sharp lance makes a hole in your armour. You are in luck. The armour stops the lance in time. You fall to the ground, winded. Take one Life Point off your score.

Brodric stops his horse. He leaps off. He draws his broad-sword. You stagger to your feet. Prepare to fight on at **54**.

42

You go into the Computer Room. You know that you are going to the Middle Ages in Britain, but you do not know the Nexus Point that Brodric has chosen. You run a computer program to look at Nexus Points in the Middle Ages. The computer comes up with these Nexus Points in the Middle Ages:

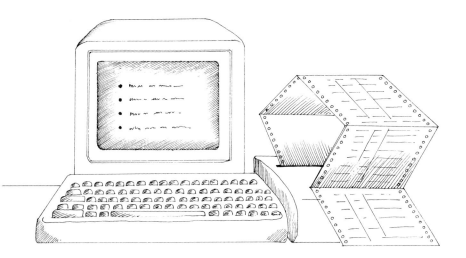

- The Battle of Hastings
- The murder of Thomas a Becket
- The Battle of Agincourt
- The Battle of Bosworth Field

You think that these four Nexus Points are the most important events in the Middle Ages and that they are most likely to be visited by Brodric.

You tell the computer to print out a Time Line showing other important dates in the Middle Ages. Write down *Middle Ages Time Line* and story number **50** on your Equipment List. You can look at the list at any time at **50**.

Now you can go to the Library – **51** – or the Equipment Room – **111**.

43

Wrong! Take one Life Point off your score! Then go to **92**.

44

You tell Henry to use the longbow. This is good advice. The longbow is an important weapon in this battle. Add one Life Point to your score. You also get a longbow for yourself. Write *Longbow* down on your Equipment List. Then go to **40**.

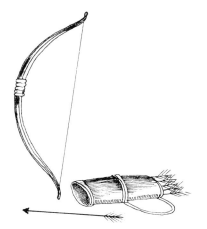

45

Brodric's man, dressed as the Saxon Carl, is going to stop the arrow killing King Harold. As you watch you see him hold up his shield. An arrow thunks into it! You turn and say to the man next to you, 'Look, that's King Harold!'. In one movement he sets his arrow and fires. Will the arrow find its mark? The arrow runs true and Harold falls clutching his eye. The Saxons lose hope and the tide of the battle turns to the Normans. The Saxon Carl turns his horse away shouting as he goes, 'We will find another way!'.

You are sad and sick to see a man killed like that, let alone a king. Yet there was no other way. You had to let History take its path. The Past must not be changed. This is your job. You turn away with a heavy heart. The Battle of Hastings was a very important Nexus Point. The Normans changed life in Britain. If William had not won, Britain would not be as it is in your own time.

Now you must go forward in Time to the next Nexus Point to confront Brodric. Add two Life Points to your score and go to **46**.

46

When you get back to the Time Machine a light is flashing. There is a message for you. You play it back.

SOS SOS SOS SOS SOS Urgent message from Time Leader. One of the Time Patrol has been taken. He is locked in the dungeon of Baron Baric in the year 1102. You must go to help.

If you want to help, go to **56**. If you think that there is no time to help because you have to get to the next Nexus Point, go to **12**.

47

In these Times they do not have strong concrete. Nor do they know about putting long steel rods into concrete and in any case they can't make steel. They do have mortar which they use to keep the bricks together but this will not give the walls the support they need. The master builder laughs and tells you not to be silly. Lose one Life Point and go back to **16**.

48

1485 is the date of the Battle of Bosworth Field at the end of the Wars of the Roses. Lose one Life Point and go to **106**.

49

Throw your dice and work out your Fighting Skill points. Prepare to meet:

BRODRIC AT BOSWORTH
FIGHTING SKILLS 25

If you win, go to **64**. If you lose, go to **81**.

MIDDLE AGES TIME LINE

King	Date	Event
William I (the Conqueror)	1066	Norman invasion Battle of Hastings King Harold killed Norman castles Domesday Book Norman manors Norman churches
William II	1087	Monasteries
Henry I	1100	Barons at peace under a strong king
Stephen	1135	Wars between Matilda and Stephen Barons at war too!
Henry II	1154 1170	Better laws Thomas a Becket murdered at Canterbury
Richard I	1189	Crusades
John	1199	Magna Carta Robin Hood?
Henry III	1216	More Barons wars First parliament
Edward I	1272	Wales conquered Castles built
Edward II	1307	Scottish defeat English
Edward III	1327	French wars The Black Death

○ Richard II	1377	Chaucer	○
○ Henry IV	1399	Henry IV takes Richard's throne	○
○ Henry V	1413	Henry V becomes king	○
	1415	Battle of Agincourt	
○ Henry VI	1422	Wars of the Roses	○
○		York: white rose	
		Lancaster: red rose	
○ Edward IV	1461	First printing press	○
○ Edward V	1483	Edward V murdered in tower	○
○		with brother	○
Richard III	1483	Richard III becomes king	
○	1485	Battle of Bosworth Field	○
○ Henry VII	1485	Tudors begin	○

51

You go to the Library and look up the Battle of Hastings.
You think that this is the first Nexus Point you will visit. You
find out that in these Times England was ruled by King
Harold. People in England were mainly Saxon. The French
Duke William of Normandy claimed that the Crown of
England belonged to him. The Normans were preparing to
invade England. You make some notes about Norman life
and the Battle of Hastings. Then you go to the Equipment
Room – **111**.

52

Right! Add one Life Point to your score! You take a white
rose with you from the garden of the Time Patrol Centre.
Write *White Rose* down on your Equipment List. Then go to
92.

53

This is not good news. In an Ordeal by Water the person is tied up and thrown into the river. If they float they are guilty. If they sink they are innocent (but drowned!). You cannot win this Ordeal! Lose one Life Point and go back to **7**!

54

A broadsword is very heavy. Every time the swords connect you are thrown to one side. Turning, ducking and thrusting makes you tired. The armour is also very heavy. After a short while you are both worn out. Who will win?

Throw your dice and prepare to meet:

THE BLACK KNIGHT ON FOOT
FIGHTING SKILLS 17

If you win, go to **67**. If you lose, go to **108**.

55

You tell Henry to use the crossbow. This is bad advice. Although the crossbow is a powerful weapon, it takes a long time to reload and it fires at a slower rate than the longbow. You should have said the longbow! Lose one Life Point and go to **40**.

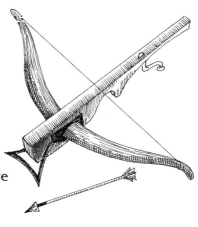

56

You go to the year 1102.
Henry I has been on the
throne for two years.
Norman rule has been a
way of life for many years.
You put aside the clothes
you wore for the invasion.
You put on a simple tunic
and leggings instead. You
hide the Time Machine
and travel to Baron Baric's
castle. You decide to go to
the market in the castle
grounds to see if you can
work out a way of freeing
your friend.

As you cross a river by a
few houses you see a mill.
It has a large wheel that
turns a grindstone. The
grindstone is used to
make wheat into flour. Just
as you are about to step
on to the path past the
mill, the Miller comes out of his house. 'Hey! Villein!', he
says. 'Come and help me with this sack of flour!' You can:

- take no notice and walk on – **104**
- ask him why he has called you a villein
  because you're not a thief – **65**
- go and help him – **85**

57

Lose two points. Pigs may live in dirty places, but they do
not carry bubonic plague. Go back to **29** and choose again.

58

The outlaw steps to one side and your blow goes past him. He steps in and strikes you on the arm. You drop your staff. Lose one Life Point and go to **30**.

59

You set sail to France. At the Battle of Agincourt the English archers stand behind pointed stakes. They wait for the French knights to ride full charge into them. Many French knights are killed by falling from their horses on to the pointed stakes.

Some of the English archers hold up two fingers at the French. Why do you think they do this? Are they showing the V sign to mean victory – go to **9** – or are they being rude – **73**?

60

No! Lose one point! The villeins are very poor. They cannot afford to let a field go to waste. There must be a reason. Go to **94**.

61

You reply in Norman French. Add one Life Point to your score. You are meant to be part of the Norman invading force and wouldn't know any English. When you have helped unload you follow the army. Go to **62**.

The Battle of Hastings is very harsh. Many men are killed. The Saxons fight well with their swords and axes. The Normans seem to be better at riding their horses. In your own time you have seen pictures of this battle in the Bayeux Tapestry. This was a picture embroidered on linen by the Normans after the battle. The real fighting is much more bloody. There is a lot of mud, screaming and terror.

An important part of the battle was the killing of the Saxon King Harold. He died when an arrow was shot into his eye. This was the last straw for the Saxon army and the Normans won the battle.

As you get nearer to Harold you see one of the Saxon nobles looking at you. The Saxon nobles were called Carls. This Carl is looking at your wrist. Then you see that you have made a very stupid mistake. You have left your watch on! The Carl charges at you on his horse. 'Brodric said that one of the Time Patrol would be here!', he sneers. The Carl is really one of the enemies of the Future who is trying to change Time. He is trying to stop the arrow reaching Harold.

You take out your own weapon and prepare to meet:

SAXON CARL
FIGHTING SKILLS 12

Throw your dice. Add up the total. Then use the Adventure Sheet in the back of the book to see if you have won or lost. If you win, go to **103**. If you lose, go to **27**.

63

You will have to be careful. You do not want to change History! You must not tell him any modern facts. You look at the drawing. 'What you need is a support that takes the weight of the walls outwards as well as down', you say. 'Perhaps a pillar that takes some of the weight. You could put it outside the walls.'

flying buttress

The builder looks at you! He gets very excited and looks at the drawing. He only needs this one hint. Over the next few weeks he develops the idea of a flying buttress. He forgets that it was not his idea! Add two Life Points to your score.

Now it is time for you to go to Canterbury – go to **107**.

64

You let the arrow fly. You thank your lucky stars for all the training you had when you joined the Time Patrol. The Time Leader knew that archery might help you in the Middle Ages. Brodric pulls the trigger of his machine gun, but your arrow flies into it. The gun fires instead in the direction of his Time Machine which is hidden behind a bush. It bursts into flame. You race over to Brodric and snatch the gun from his hands.

As you run to your own Time Machine you see that the tide of the battle is turning. King Richard III has been slain! You jump into your Time Machine.

Brodric is left stranded in 1485! You set the controls to go back to the Time Patrol Centre. Go to **84**.

65

'Who are you calling a thief?!', you shout. The miller looks at you as if you are mad. You have made a mistake. Lose one Life Point and go to **85**.

66

You put bleach in the water supplies. The Black Death was not carried by water. You have made the water undrinkable with your bleach. Lose one Life Point and choose again – **88**.

67

At last one of your blows crashes into the Black Knight. He falls to the ground, stunned. He lies on the ground like an upside-down turtle! You lift his visor and hold the point of your sword to his face. The Black Knight says, 'Very well! You win this time, but we will meet again'.

Add one Life Point to your score and go to **68**.

68

Brodric is giving bad advice to King Henry so that England will lose the Battle of Agincourt and History will be changed.

Now that you have beaten the Black Knight you can give the right advice to the King. You can tell him to take a large force of knights in armour but only a few archers – go to **13** – or you can tell him to take a large force of archers as well as the knights – **95**.

69

You do not know which Nexus Point you are going to yet! Lose one Life Point and go to the Computer Room – **42**.

70

You begin to tire! You slip and the axeman raises his axe for the final strike! Lose two points. You roll to one side and get to your feet.

You must get out of this Time. You turn and run. Go to **75**.

71

The Abbot gives you a funny look. Why are you praying in the language of the King's court? Lose one Life Point and choose again at **107**.

72

You scramble down the stairs and out of the Keep. When you get to the outer bailey you find that the drawbridge over the moat is up! You scramble up to the battlements. You take no notice of any wound you might have. You throw the axe away. You dive into the moat and swim ashore. A frantic sprint takes you to the place where you have hidden the Time Machine. You quickly set the time for the year 2167. You are safe!

When you get back to the Time Patrol Centre, the Time Leader is waiting for you. 'You haven't much time!', she says. 'Quickly! Get ready to go to the next Nexus Point!'

If you have any wounds, the Time Patrol Centre's doctor cleans them up. Then you collect some more costumes. You are going to visit the time of Henry II and the murder of Thomas a Becket. At last you are ready. You get into the Time Machine. Which year are you going to? You can go to 1485 – **48** – or 1170 – **106**.

73

The two-finger V sign that is used in your own time came from the English archers. It is not a rude insult in the Middle Ages. The archers show the French two fingers because they use these fingers to draw back the bow. If the French capture any English archers in battle, they cut off their first two fingers so that they can no longer use their bows.

By showing their two fingers the English archers are mocking the French. In years to come, the two-finger V sign was to become a rude insult! Go to **80**.

74

1415 is the wrong battle. It is the Battle of Agincourt, not the Battle of Hastings. Lose one Life Point. Go to **35** and choose again.

75

The crowd lets you go. They think you have done well against such a huge man. They block the path of the soldiers chasing you. You run to the Time Machine. You ask yourself why you joined in the sports competition. When will you learn?! Well, you have ended up with a useful axe anyway. Write *Battle-axe* on your Equipment List. You quickly set the Time Machine to the year 1170 – the year of the murder of Thomas a Becket. Go to **110**.

76

The guard will not do anything a mere villein says. Also, you do not have time to talk to him before the soldiers catch up with you. Lose one Life Point and go to **18**.

You go over to the archery contest. You watch for a while. You take note of the distance and the direction of the wind. You ask one of the archers if you can borrow his bow. You try out the bow. Then you put all the information you have gathered into your pocket computer. The computer tells you where to aim and how far back to pull the bow. You score a bullseye! But someone is watching you! Go to **5**.

78

You stand aside and let them go by. Go to **83**.

79

You do not know which Nexus Point you are going to yet! How can you know what you need? Lose one Life Point and go to the Computer Room – **42**.

The French knights charge! Do you have the Longbow? Check your Equipment List. If not, go back to **44** and get it. Then come back here. You can use the Longbow to help defeat the French.

You and the others firing longbows send flight after flight of arrows into the French lines. The arrows fall like rain. Hundreds of French knights are killed. They are wearing very thick armour to try to keep out the arrows. This makes them clumsy and slow.

You join the English knights. You dismount and help the archers. You and the other knights fight with swords. The French do not have an army that can do this. They only have many knights, a few crossbow men and peasants who do not really want to fight!

Agincourt is a victory for England and Henry V becomes King of a large part of France. The English lose all of France again in years to come. You have helped to keep the balance of power between France and England. You return to your Time Machine and go to the year 2167. Go to **90**.

81

Before you can let the arrow fly Brodric fires. Bullets spray around you. The archer next to you is killed. Lose two Life Points and throw again at **49**.

82

The figure in green steps out in front of you. He is an outlaw. If the village baron or lord of the manor is unkind people sometimes run away. They often become outlaws. This man looks hungry. He says he will fight you with a staff for some of the beans you have. He hands you a thick staff of wood, and holds his own up ready. Prepare to meet:

FOREST OUTLAW
FIGHTING SKILLS 10

Now throw your dice and work out your Fighting Skill points. You have been trained in the use of many weapons but a staff is not one of them. You hold the staff up, but the outlaw cracks you on the shin! You rush at him with your staff held high for a wild blow! If you win the fight, go to **14**. If you lose, go to **58**.

As he goes by the Black Knight hisses, 'Too late, Time Patrol! The Archbishop dies!'. Lose one Life Point.

When you get to Canterbury you find that Archbishop Thomas a Becket has been killed. Some knights have burst into the cathedral and struck him down. They said that King Henry told them to do it. It is true that the King, in a fit of temper, said that he wished someone would rid him of Thomas. Brodric, also known as the Black Knight, has used this as an excuse to murder Thomas a Becket.

You make the long journey back to your Time Machine. You return to your own time. You go to visit Canterbury Cathedral. There you see a shrine marking the spot where Becket was murdered. If only you could have stopped the murder!

Just then the Time Leader steps up to you! You are surprised to see her. 'You have not failed!' she tells you. 'That Nexus Point was a complex one. Brodric made a mistake. When Becket was killed it changed the power struggle between the State and the Church. Thomas a Becket became a saint. So his murder actually changed the course of History. We should not change it back! Now, stop standing about feeling sorry for yourself. You are needed in the Middle Ages again!' Go to **86**.

You arrive at the Time Patrol Centre. The Time Leader is there to meet you. Add two points to your score. You learn that Brodric has been killed at the Battle of Bosworth Field. Henry Tudor has become King Henry VII. The Wars of the Roses are over and a new line of kings and queens has begun. They are called the Tudors and they are going to lead England to great things in the future. Go to **125**.

85

The miller thinks you are one of the common people of a nearby village. The common people are called villeins. The villeins have to work for the lord of the manor. They have to plough his fields and give him crops. A villein cannot leave the lord's land unless he is needed to fight for the lord. This is called the feudal system.

The miller is a freeman. He has saved money to buy his freedom. Now he is telling you to help him. You do what he says. You want to get to the castle. People must think you are one of them.

The miller is not a bad man. When you have helped move his flour sacks, he gives you some bread and cheese. Add one point to your score. Write down *Bread and Cheese* on your Equipment List. You thank him and walk on. When you get to the fields you need to pick something to sell at the market.

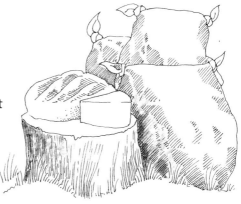

There are three fields. One has wheat, one has beans and the other does not seem to be growing anything. Why do you think this is? If you think it is empty because the people have forgotten to plant any seed, go to **60**. If you think it has been left for a reason, go to **94**. If you think it has been left as a playing field, go to **97**.

86

A lot has happened since you were on the road to Canterbury. In 1215, the barons made King John sign the Magna Carta. The Magna Carta listed the rights of the barons and was the start of justice for people. One of the things it said was that a 'freeman' could not be put in prison or hung without a fair trial. Peasants, who were almost like slaves to their landlords, were not granted these rights. They were not happy about this and, together with the unfair taxes they had to pay, it may have led to the Peasants Revolt much later, in 1381. The Revolt ended when Wat Tyler, one of the leaders of the revolt, was killed by the Lord Mayor of London and the peasants lost heart.

Since you went to Canterbury, the first parliament has been held. It was held in 1265 in the reign of Henry III. It was a meeting of knights and barons and was the beginning of everyone having a say in the way the country is run. After that, Edward I defeated the Welsh and castles were built to defend and hold Wales. Edward II was defeated by the Scottish at Bannockburn. Scotland was separate from England for more than two hundred years after Bannockburn. After their success with the English, the Scottish invaded Ireland in the North, at Ulster.

You have not got time to visit these places and events. Instead, the Time Leader sends you to 1348. Edward III is on the throne. England is in the middle of a long war with France. The two countries have been at war on and off for many years. In years to come this was to be known as the Hundred Years War.

Something worse than war has come to Britain. Brodric and his evil men have been quiet for many years. Now a terrible illness has come to Europe from Asia. It is a bubonic plague called the Black Death. Brodric did not start the Black Death but he is doing all he can to spread it. He and his men are going from town to town putting the germs that cause the plague into the water of the towns and villages. You have to try and stop this.

What will you use to fight the Black Death? Go to **88**.

87

1170 is the year of the murder of Thomas a Becket. This is the wrong Nexus Point. Lose one Life Point. Go to **35** and choose again.

88

You can choose from bleach to clean up the water – go to **66** – or antibiotics to fight the infection causing the plague – **28**.

89

At last the axeman begins to tire. He slips and you raise the axe above your head. He cries 'Craven!'. You have won! You know that the Baron will not kill him, and at least you are safe.

You must get out of this Time. You turn and run. Go to **75**.

90

The Time Leader is very pleased with you. 'That was a good bit of work', she says. 'You made sure that History didn't get changed. You gave the King some advice but you let History take its course. The less we change the better.' Add one Life Point to your score.

The Time Leader tells you that Brodric is still active in the Middle Ages. The English have now left France and many soldiers have come home. They are used to war and the barons have got them to start trouble. This trouble leads to the Wars of the Roses and the Battle of Bosworth Field. This is your next Nexus Point.

After reading up about the Wars of the Roses in the Library, you go to your Time Machine. You have found out that the two sides fighting against each other are called the House of Lancaster and the House of York. Each House has a rose as their sign – a white rose and a red rose.

In your own time, the two counties, Yorkshire and Lancashire, still have the signs of the white rose and the red rose. If you think the House of Lancaster has a red rose and the House of York has a white rose, go to **52**. If you think it was the other way around, go to **43**. (You might want to look at the Middle Ages Time Line on your Equipment List again.)

You choose to be a Page. You wear a short tunic and you have to wait at the table. You serve the knights and ladies with meat and mead. One of the knights is dressed all in black. He has a cruel face. He laughs when you spill some drink. Then he looks at you carefully. 'So, Time Patrol!', he says under his breath. It is Brodric, the Black Knight! He is trying to stop the English getting ready for Agincourt. You will have to meet him in battle in the tournament. You see some armour. It looks like this:

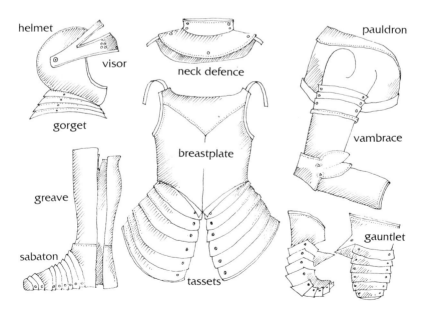

It is your size. Write down *Armour* on your Equipment List.

You will not be able to fight the Black Knight as a page. You need to choose again if you are to fight him in the tournament. When you have looked at the picture of the armour, go to **119** and choose again.

92

The Wars of the Roses are about power. The two sides are fighting about who should be on the throne. On each side there is a group of nobles with their own knights, soldiers and so on. Changing sides is not uncommon, as people try to be on the side which will win. The people living in towns or villages try not to get involved. The fighting between the barons and nobles is very hard.

You start to set the Time Machine for the year of the Battle of Bosworth Field, the next Nexus Point. Suddenly a message comes in:

SOS SOS SOS SOS Go to the Tower of London 1483

You set the controls to the Tower of London in 1483. Go to **105**.

93

You reply in English. The man draws his sword. You are meant to be part of the Norman invading force. You should have spoken in Norman French. You are forced to flee and join the forces again later. Your plan is delayed. Lose two Life Points and go to **62**.

There is a reason. In the Middle Ages people did not have the fertilisers and chemicals that farmers put on the land in your own time.

They also did not know so much about how to keep the land rich and fertile. For example, they did not know that some crops put goodness back into the ground. Instead, they made the ground richer by giving it a 'rest' from farming. To do this, they left some fields empty or 'fallow' each year. This made the soil in those fields more fertile for the next year's planting.

You go to the field of beans. The field is marked out in strips. Each villein in the village has a strip of land to farm. You take a few beans from each strip. Then you walk into the forest.

You have not gone very far when you see something move in the trees. At first you think that it is a deer. Many deer are found in the forest in these Times. Then you see that it is a person. It has a green tunic on. You get very excited! Could this be the famous Robin Hood? Go to **25** if you think the answer is yes. Go to **37** if you think the answer is no.

95

You tell Henry to take a large force of archers as well as the knights. This is good advice. The archers will be very useful in battle. Add one Life Point to your score and go to **96**.

96

The archers of England play a key part in the Battle of Agincourt. They are able to send flight after flight of arrows into the French as they charge. There are two kinds of bows which the archers can use. You have to give Henry some advice about which kind his archers should use. Do you advise him to use the longbow – go to **44** – or the crossbow – **55**?

97

No! Lose one point! The people of Norman times could not afford to let a field go to waste. They did not need a playing field because they played games on the common land where the animals grazed. Go to **94**.

98

You choose to be a Knight. Do you have both Armour and Weapons? Check that you have both on your Equipment List. If you do not you will have to go to **119** and become a Page or a Squire for a while to get them. If you do have them both you can get ready to meet the Black Knight in combat. Go to **102**.

99

This is the best of a bad bunch. (Look at the others at **53** and **118** which are worse! Do not take the points off your score if you choose Ordeal by Combat first.)

In an Ordeal by Combat you have to fight the man who accused you. You have to fight the baron's man.

He is very big and looks quick on his feet. You are both given a shield and an axe. You have to fight until one person gives up. When he gives up he shouts 'Craven!'. Then he is put to death! You will have to win! Prepare to meet:

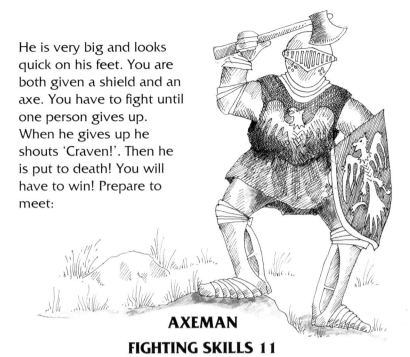

AXEMAN
FIGHTING SKILLS 11

You circle around the Axeman. He strikes out with a mighty blow. You bring your shield up just in time. The axe crashes on to your shield. You fall to the ground from the force of the blow. You scramble up and return the blow. The axeman ducks. You fight on like this for nearly an hour until both your shields are cut and split. Throw your dice and work out your Fighting Skill points. If you win, go to **89**. If you lose, go to **70**.

100

That night the Friar tells his story. He wears a grey robe and is a follower of St Francis. Friars travel about and are well loved for their kindness. The Friar tells of his travels to the Holy Land. This is where Jesus Christ lived and gave people his teachings. He shows a piece of palm tree from the Holy Land. Pilgrims who have been to the Holy Land and have a piece of palm leaf are called Palmers.

The Friar tells of the fighting that went on during the Crusades. In the Crusades knights and soldiers from England, France and other places in Europe went to the Middle East. There they tried to capture Jerusalem. He tells of a cruel man – the Black Knight – who killed and hurt women and children in the fighting. He shows a strange shape that was drawn on the Black Knight's shield. It looks like a picture of a Time Machine!

The people of 1170 do not understand what it is. You do – the Black Knight must be Brodric. He must have been trying to change the Crusades!

You fall asleep to dream about the Black Knight. The next day you travel on. Go on to the next evening – **117**.

101

You stand in front of the horses. They gallop on and you are pushed into the mud. Go to **83**.

102

The King has said that all the knights must be in full battle armour for the tournament. Sometimes lighter armour is used in mock battles called jousts but the King wants the knights to practise for the real battle against the French.

You get into your armour. You have to be helped on to your horse as the armour is so heavy. The horse is a huge shire horse. He also has armour and cloth to protect him.

You are on one side of a wooden fence called a 'tilt'. The Black Knight is on the other side. The idea is to charge at each other with your lances and knock your opponent off his horse. This is called 'tilting'.

All the knights have been told to blunt the ends of their lances for the tournament. But the Black Knight has kept his lance sharp! He sneers at you. 'Come and meet your death!', he shouts. Then he shuts the visor of his helmet with a clang. He spurs his horse and levels his lance. Horse, rider and lance thunder down at you! You just have time to close your own visor and spur your warhorse forward!

Throw your dice and prepare to meet:

THE BLACK KNIGHT ON HORSEBACK
FIGHTING SKILLS 20

If you win, go to **11**. If you lose, go to **41**.

103

The Carl crashes his horse into you. You stagger but you manage to swing up at him. He dodges your blow. Then he rides away at a gallop. He puts himself and his horse in front of Harold. Go to **45**.

104

You take no notice and walk on. The miller runs after you. 'Come and help at once or I'll call the Baron's soldiers', he shouts. You do not want to meet any soldiers right now. You go back to help him. Lose one Life Point and go to **85**.

You arrive inside a damp, dark hole of a room. There is a drip, drip, drip of cold water from the roof. The walls have slime growing on them. Rats sniff and scamper around the room. The door is open.

As you step out you hear a scream. It sounds like a child. You run towards that scream of pain. You see Brodric coming out of a cell. He runs away down the passage. The screams stop. You go into the cell. There, on the dirty floor, are two boys. They are crouched in the corner. Blood seeps from their clothes. You are too late! They are dead! One of them is 12-year-old King Edward V. He has been locked up in the Tower by his Uncle Richard. Edward V's reign has lasted for only three months from April to June 1483. The other boy is his brother.

It is possible that their uncle has ordered the murder so that he can become king. Such were the times of the Wars of the Roses.

You are thinking about these things as a shadow is cast over you. 'So!', a nasty voice says. 'I have found a killer!' It is the Jailer! He knows very well that you have not killed the boys, but he can make it look as though it was you. He comes towards you. He is a massive man with a huge belly. He holds a rusty dagger. You will have to get past him to escape. Go to **112**.

You decide to set the Time Machine to the year 1170 but you make a mistake in setting the time. You punch in 1140, not 1170. You are taken to the time of King Stephen. This is a time of wars and hardship. Brodric has been up to mischief. He has had the heir to the throne killed at sea. Stephen and Matilda are fighting for the throne.

Meanwhile the barons in their castles can do what they want. They are cruel and hard. They make war on each other and the people have to work hard to give taxes to the barons to pay for the wars. The only time there is a holiday is on a Holy Day. These are like Christmas Day, May Day or Midsummer Eve. Some of these days are from the Christian religion. Others are left over from the old pagan times when the Earth, trees and nature were thought to be gods. You have arrived on May Day. Sports competitions are being held on the green. You can take part in an archery contest – **77** – or a wrestling contest – **113**.

107

Just before you go, the Abbot asks all the pilgrims to pray together. You happen to be sitting next to him in the church. You have to decide which language you will pray in:

- English – go to **33**
- Latin – **116**
- Norman French – **71**

108

One of the Black Knight's blows crashes into you. You fall to the ground, stunned. Take one Life Point off your score.

You must win this fight if you are to stop Brodric from changing History. You shake your head. You try to get up. Go to **54** and try again.

109

That night you hear the Wool Merchant's story. The wool merchant is a woman who sells good English wool to people from Flanders (Belgium). There it is woven into fine cloth. She is a rich and powerful woman. She gives you a piece of fine cloth. Write *Woollen Cloth* on your Equipment List.

The wool merchant tells stories about the court of Henry II. She says that Thomas a Becket is often arguing with the King. The Church and State want to be more powerful than each other. She says that there is a knight in the court who is always making trouble. He wears black and has a strange mark on his shield.

Before you go to sleep that night you see a man sitting by the fire. He is writing on parchment. He says his name is Chaucer. You wonder if this is Geoffrey Chaucer. He wrote a book called the Canterbury Tales. This book became famous in future times. It was about the lives and times of the pilgrims on their way to Canterbury. Then you remember that Geoffery Chaucer died in 1400. This Chaucer cannot be the same one! It must be someone else. Perhaps it is Chaucer's great-grandfather! The next day you travel on. Go on to the next evening – **117**.

It is the year 1170. King Henry II has been on the throne for 16 years. He is a strong king. He has made the barons stop fighting. He is sometimes called The Lawgiver because he has made new laws. He has introduced the system of trial by a jury of twelve peers. (A peer is someone who is the same kind of person as the person being tried.) This system is still used in your own time.

In these Times the Church is very rich. It is also very powerful. The abbots, who are the heads of the monasteries or abbeys, are trying to control the King and the barons. The Head of the Church is the Archbishop of Canterbury. In 1170, the Archbishop is Thomas a Becket. He has very strong views and disagrees with King Henry. To get to this Nexus Point, you will have to visit Canterbury in Kent. First of all, you need to look as if you are part of the Church. Brodric and his men will be looking out for you. You can choose to pretend to be a Monk – go to **10** – or a Nun – go to **21**.

111

If you have been to the Library already add one Life Point to your score. If you have not been to the Library yet lose one Life Point. Go there now (**51**) and then come back here. You can choose to be:

- a Norman Knight – **22**
- a Norman Lady – **23**
- a Norman Archer – **24**

Throw your dice and work out your Fighting Skill points. Now prepare to meet the:

JAILER
FIGHTING SKILLS 10

If you win, go to **114**. If you lose, go to **4**.

113

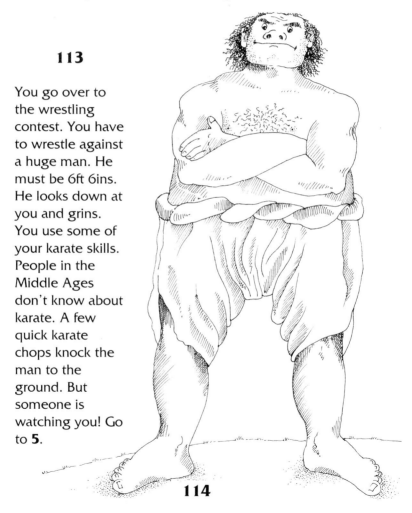

You go over to the wrestling contest. You have to wrestle against a huge man. He must be 6ft 6ins. He looks down at you and grins. You use some of your karate skills. People in the Middle Ages don't know about karate. A few quick karate chops knock the man to the ground. But someone is watching you! Go to **5**.

114

You try to dodge past the jailer. He slashes out with his knife but he is too fat to be fast. You duck and run out of

the door. You race back to your Time Machine. Richard III
will pay for this murder! You must go quickly to the next
Nexus Point. You set the Time Machine to 1485, the year of
the Battle of Bosworth Field. Go to **26**.

115

You charge and send one of the men crashing to the
ground. You swing the axe at the other. You catch him with
the flat of the axe and he falls, stunned, next to his friend.
Add one Life Point to your score. You run out of the door.
Go to **72**.

116

Well done! The Church uses Latin in these Times as it was
the language spoken by many at the time of Jesus Christ.
Latin is still sometimes used by churches in your own time.
Add one Life Point to your score. Then leave for
Canterbury. Go to **117**.

117

There are many people on the pilgrimage. In the evening
you all gather around the fire and tell each other stories.
You can choose to listen to the stories of:

- the Baker – go to **36**
- the Friar – **100**
- or the Wool Merchant – **109**
- if you have heard all three stories – go to **120**

All the stories will help you on your mission.

118

This is bad news. In an Ordeal by Fire the person has to carry a piece of red hot iron for three paces. Then their hands are bound up. If there are no blisters on their hands after three days, they are innocent. You cannot wait for three days! Lose one Life Point and go back to **7**!

119

You can choose to be:

- a Page – go to **91**
- a Squire – **3**
- a Knight – **98**

120

You should have heard all three tales by now. Add two Life Points if you have. If you have not, go back to **117** and choose a tale which you have not heard.

When you have heard all the tales, you can carry on towards Canterbury. You are only two miles away now. Suddenly you hear the sound of horses. You see a small group of men riding quickly. They draw up from behind and you see that one is a knight dressed in black. He seems to stare at you as he rushes past.

You can either let them go by – **78** – or try to stop them – **101**.

Add one point. By killing the rats with poison you save some people from the Black Death. Rats are one of the main ways in which the Black Death is spread. Fleas from infected rats get on to humans and bite them. The flea bites put the bacteria (germs) that cause the plague into the person's blood. In these Times most people have fleas! Fleas are very small and difficult to kill. It is better to try and kill the rats.

The plague kills many people. Think about ten people you know. Now imagine that four of them die. That is how it is during the Black Death. About four out of every ten people catch it and die. In parts of Europe seven out of ten people are killed. In some villages and manors hardly anyone is left alive. The Black Death lasts for 20 years.

As so many people die during the Black Death, new laws are passed to stop people leaving the land they farm for food. Many farmers turn to keeping sheep rather than growing vegetables. This is because you need more people to till the land than you do to rear sheep.

The Time Leader will be angry that you interfered with History by saving some people from the Black Death. But you know that you have not changed Time. You have only been able to save a few people.

You will have to leave now. You can only do so much. The next Nexus Point is becoming urgent. Get back into the Time Machine and go forward to **122**.

122

Do you have the Woollen Cloth? Check your Equipment List. If you do not have it, you will have to go back to **109** to get it and then come back here. If you do have it, you can use it shortly to make yourself some clothes. You go to the year 1415. King Henry V is on the throne. He is a strong king but he is often away fighting the French. In 1415 King Henry fights the Battle of Agincourt, an important battle in the Hundred Years War with France.

You arrive in the year 1415 just as King Henry is gathering his army together to invade France. A few weeks before the battle there is a tournament so that the army can practise their knightly skills. King Henry, his knights, nobles, foot-soldiers and archers all meet at a noble's castle. Go to **119**.

123

What? He is fully armed and the soldiers are upon you. Lose one Life Point and go to **18**.

124

Add one Life Point to your score. Go to **42**.

125

The Time Leader tells you to take a holiday. You have played a part in keeping the History of the Middle Ages as it should be. You have covered a long period of time – more than 400 years from 1066 to 1485. If you would like to help the Time Patrol again, look out for more books like this one!

GOODBYE FOR NOW AND GOOD LUCK!

THE BLACK KNIGHT ADVENTURE SHEET

Name...... Oliver Lane ....

Each time you fight you must work out your Fighting Skill points.

| You have already been given some Fighting Skill points for each fight. | + | Throw both your dice and write down the total number you have thrown. | = | Add your numbers together to find your total Fighting Skill points. |

Skills points given + Dice throw = Your total Fighting Skill points

You win if you have the same or more Fighting Skill points than your enemy.

You lose if you have fewer Fighting Skill points than your enemy.

Enemy	Your Skill points	Dice throw	Your total Fighting Skill points	Enemy's Fighting Skill points	Win/Lose
Saxon Carl	6 +	5	= 11	12	lose
Forest Outlaw	6 +	10	= 16	10	win
Baron's guards	10 +	6	= 16	15	win
Axeman	6 +	8	= 14	11	win
Black Knight on horseback	14 +	8	= 22	20	win
Black Knight on foot	12 +	9	= 21	17	win
Jailer	8 +	5	= 13	10	win
Brodric at Bosworth	18 +	7	= 25	25	win

Life Points	Equipment List	Story Number
25		79
24	Middle Age time line	50
23		
24		
21	Bread+	
23	Chees	85
24	castle plan	50
25		
24	cloth bag	18
26	Dattle	75
27	Axe	
29	woolen	
30	cloth	109
32	wepons	
31		
30	armor	
31		
32	long	
33	bow	
34	whright	
35	Rose	
36		
37		
39		